Gratefully presented to

Pastor Peter Hanson

by

Patricia Jessen

on

February 11, 1997

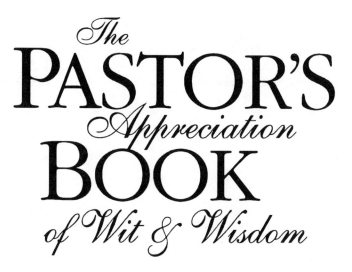

# The PASTOR'S *Appreciation* BOOK *of Wit & Wisdom*

*Compiled by Douglas J. Brouwer*

Harold Shaw Publishers
Wheaton, Illinois

Copyright 1992 by Harold Shaw Publishers
Originally published under the title *I Heard It at the Potluck*

Unless otherwise indicated, all Scripture quotations are taken from *The Holy Bible: New International Version.* Copyright © 1973, 1978, 1984 by the International Bible Society. Used by permission of Zondervan Publishing House. All rights reserved.

Other Bible versions used are as follows: RSV, The Revised Standard Version; TLB, The Living Bible; KJV, The King James Version.

Cover design by David LaPlaca
Compiled by Douglas J. Brouwer
ISBN 0-87788-641-5

**Library of Congress Cataloging-in-Publication Data**

I heard it at the potluck
    The pastor's appreciation book of wit and wisdom / Douglas J. Brouwer, compiler and editor.
        p.   cm.
    Originally published under title: I heard it at the potluck. ©1993.
    ISBN 0-87788-641-5
    1. Church—Quotations, maxims, etc. 2. Clergy—Quotations, maxims, etc. I. Brouwer, Douglas J.
    [BV600.2.I3 1995]
    202—dc20                                                                95-40734
                                                                            CIP

02  01  00  99  98  97  96

10  9  8  7  6  5  4  3

# CONTENTS

## Leaders of the Flock

## Sunday Morning

## Church Life

## Potluck

# LEADERS
# OF THE
# FLOCK

# Job Description

Now the overseer must be above reproach, the husband of but one wife, temperate, self-controlled, respectable, hospitable, able to teach, not given to drunkenness, not violent but gentle, not quarrelsome, not a lover of money.

*1 Timothy 3:2-3*

The definition of a popular preacher: one who knows the difference between preaching and meddling.

*Anonymous*

There is a saying among physicians that the doctor who is his own doctor has a fool for a doctor. If those entrusted with the care of the body cannot be trusted to look after their own bodies, far less can those entrusted with the care of souls look after their own souls, which are even more complex than bodies and have a correspondingly greater capacity for self-deceit.

*Eugene H. Peterson,* Working the Angles

In the typical small or middle-sized congregation, the most highly-prized competence in a minister is the ability to accept the role as the local expert in the Christian view of death.

*Lyle E. Schaller,* Getting Things Done

The ideal pastor:
is always casual but never underdressed;
is warm and friendly but not too familiar;
is humorous but not funny;
calls on his [or her] members but is never out of the office;
is an expository preacher but always preaches on the family;
is profound but comprehensible;
condemns sin but is always positive;
has a family of ordinary people who never sin;
has two eyes, one brown and the other blue!

*Kent and Barbara Hughes,* Liberating Ministry from the Success Syndrome

A minister should be a person who can hold her or his own in any community and be able to give leadership in lifting moral standards and raising human vision.

*James I. McCord*

I was at a Red Cross bloodmobile to donate my annual pint and being asked a series of questions by a nurse to see if there was any reason for disqualification. The final question on the list was, "Do you engage in hazardous work?" I said, "Yes." She was . . . a little surprised, for I was wearing a clerical collar by which she could identify me as a pastor. . . . She smiled, ignored my answer and marked the no on her questionnaire, saying, "I don't mean that kind of hazardous."

*Eugene H. Peterson,* A Long Obedience

An introverted person who is highly productive will often be more successful than a more extroverted person who is less productive.

*Lyle E. Schaller*

God doesn't call us to success, only to faithfulness.

*Anonymous*

Ordination confers a whole set of expectations. Congregations are, for example, no longer impressed by my growth on the job. When a congregation receives a callow youth from seminary [for an internship year] and then says good-bye to that person as a polished pastor, they can be proud of him (and her) as well as themselves. When a congregation receives an ordained pastor, they expect to get their money's worth.

*Douglas J. Brouwer,* Reformed Journal

I think I discovered for myself the deepest paradox of self control. It is this: One way to get in control of one's life is surrender to unconditional love. The love that accepts me with no reference to my deserving. I have to get back to that surrender now and then or I lose control again to the demon of other people's approval.

*Lewis B. Smedes,* A Pretty Good Person

If you are replacing a Super Christian and have tremendous expectations heaped upon you, spend some time looking at your own personality, your own gifts, and determine what God wants of you in your particular situation. Be willing to disappoint others' expectations. . . . Other people (such as those in the new congregation) also have to take God's surprises in stride, and one of those surprises may be you!

*Jill Briscoe,* Renewal on the Run

Well-educated ministers are not individuals who can tell you exactly who God is, where good and evil are and how to travel from this world to the next, but people whose articulate not-knowing makes them free to listen to the voice of God in the words of people, in the events of the day and in the books containing the life experience of men and women from other places and other times. In short, learned ignorance makes one able to receive the word from others and the Other with great attention.

*Henri J.M. Nouwen,* Reaching Out

He who teaches the Bible is never a scholar; he is always a student.

*Vern McLellan*

In the sixties, the top three criteria for the success of a new church were location, location, location. But in the nineties, the top three criteria are clearly the pastor, the pastor, the pastor.

*Lyle E. Schaller*

The Christian messenger cannot think too highly of his Prince, or too humbly of himself.

*Charles Caleb Colton*

# Advice to Shepherds

A suggested prayer for preachers: O Lord, fill my heart with worthwhile stuff, and nudge me when I've said enough.

*Anonymous*

Always appoint people who earn a lot more than you do to the Personnel Committee.

*Fred R. Anderson*

Never resign on Monday!

*Anonymous*

Whatever happens to you, never give up praying. It would be like giving up breathing.

*Henri J.M. Nouwen, seminary commencement address*

Go your way; behold, I send you out as lambs in the midst of wolves. Carry no purse, no bag, no sandals; and salute no one on the road. . . . Whenever you enter a town and they receive you, eat what is set before you; heal the sick in it and say to them, "The kingdom of God has come near to you."

*Luke 10:3-4, 8-9, RSV*

The person who is never criticized is not breathing.

*Vern McLellan*

People assume that preachers of any age are unacquainted with the less savory aspects of human behavior and are easily shocked by confession of any species of sin more spectacular than an occasional errant thought. . . . When the day comes that a parishioner makes an appointment to "talk over a personal problem" you must quell your excitement.

*Charles Merrill Smith,* How to Become A Bishop Without Being Religious

To keep yourself from feeling indispensable, just remember: If you were to die today, your body wouldn't be cold before people would be jockeying to get on the next search committee.

*Fred R. Anderson*

When young, consider that one day you will be old and when old, remember you were once young.

*Jo Petty,* Apples of Gold

Be in your last parish by the time you are 50.

*Anonymous*

Don't refuse to accept criticism; get all the help you can.

*Proverbs 23:12, TLB*

Coming back to the old parish is a kind of denial that the pastoral relationship is over.

*Douglas J. Brouwer,* Perspectives

Don't let the door hit you on the way out.

*Anonymous*

Do your grieving [about leaving] in your old parish.

*Anonymous*

Never put a married pastor in charge of the church's singles group.

*Anonymous*

The pastoral ministry is too adventuresome and demanding to be sustained by trivial, psychological self-improvement advice.

*Stanley Hauerwas and William Willimon,* Resident Aliens

The three rules of supervison are: Follow up, Follow up, Follow up.

*Fred R. Anderson*

We must practice what we preach.

*Sir Roger L'Estrange,* Seneca's Morals

If you leave [your parish], you may not so much as use the restroom of your old church without written permission.

*Anonymous (verbal instructions to a departing pastor)*

A man wrapped up in himself makes a very small bundle.

*Anonymous*

# Those Who Lead

To lead people, walk behind them.

*Lao-Tzu*

Every leader is being evaluated by the followers.

*Lyle E. Schaller,* Getting Things Done

Leadership is finding the parade and getting in front of it—except today there are more parades and they are smaller.

*John Naisbitt*

I am the good shepherd. The good shepherd lays down his life for the sheep.

*John 10:11*

Parishioners may see the minister as an authority figure, a father or mother figure, who is a stand-in for or representative of God. Seen in this light, the pastor is immediately the object of the universal ambivalence toward father authority and mother authority: on the one hand there is the feeling of veneration and respect; on the other hand there can be seething resentment, rebellion, and hostility.

*E. Mansell Pattison, M.D.,* Pastor and Parish

When the best leader's work is done, the people say, "We did it ourselves!"

*Lao-Tzu*

True leadership must be for the benefit of the followers, not the enrichment of the leaders. In combat, officers eat last.

*Robert Townsend,* Up the Organization

Most hierarchies are nowadays so cumbered with rules and traditions, and so bound in by public laws, that even high employees do not have to lead anywhere, in the sense of pointing out the direction and setting the pace. They simply follow precedents, obey regulations, and move at the head of the crowd. Such employees lead only in the sense that the carved wooden figurehead leads the ship.

*Peter and Hull,* The Peter Principle

Where there is no vision, the people perish.

*Proverbs 29:18, KJV*

On reserved parking spaces: If you're so bloody important, you better be the first one in the office. Besides, you'll meet a nice class of people in the employees' parking lot.

*Robert Townsend,* Up the Organization

To be lured by promises of being needed and then to be stranded is the most devastating of experiences for a minister.

*James E. Dittes,* When The People Say No

We tend to meet any new situation by reorganizing . . . and [what] a wonderful method it can be for creating the illusion of progress while producing inefficiency and demoralization.

*Petronius (circa 66 A.D.)*

If you want pure, effective, real, and lively belief, then do not use coercion to support it.

*William Lee Miller, (paraphrasing James Madison in)* The First Liberty

The Reverend Henry Ward Beecher entered Plymouth Church one Sunday and found several letters waiting for him. He opened one and found it contained the single word, "Fool!" To the congregation on Sunday he said: "I have known many an instance of a man writing a letter and forgetting to sign his name, but this is the first instance I have ever known of a man signing his name and forgetting to write the letter."

*Anonymous*

Jesus exercises the only kind of leadership that can evoke authentic community—a leadership that risks failure (and even crucifixion) by making space for other people to act.

*Parker J. Palmer,* The Active Life

You cannot help men permanently by doing for them what they could and should do for themselves.

*Abraham Lincoln*

The taller a bamboo grows, the lower it bends.

*Jo Petty,* Apples of Gold

A pastor is a leader. It is the leader's responsibility to know when it's time to leave. If the pastor waits until the people conclude that it's time for him to leave, then the pastor has become the follower.

*Edward A. White,* Saying Good-bye

Seems as if some people grow with responsibility—others just swell.

*Anonymous*

Of all vocations the Christian ministry is the most sacred, the most exacting, the most humbling.

*Sir William Robertson Nicoll*

# Pastoral Duties

The minister has only 168 hours in a week.

*Lyle E. Schaller,* The Middle-Sized Church

The pastor should always be prepared to pray, preach, and die.

*Anonymous*

The duties of the pastor: . . . to draw to Christ those who are alienated; to lead back those have been drawn away; to secure amendment of life to those who fall into sin; to preserve Christians who are whole and strong; and to urge them forward in all good.

*Martin Bucer (16th century)*

There is a danger of doing too much as well as of doing too little. Life is not for work, but work for life; and when it is carried to the extent of undermining life or unduly absorbing it, work is not praiseworthy but blameworthy.

*Ralph Turnbull*

All around us, at any hour, people show up who ask us to do something about them. In the kitchen, in the bedroom, in the shop, in the neighborhood, in the oval office, at a party, in a conversation, in a crisis, in a lull, at home, at work, in church, in politics—anywhere, everywhere, somebody may at any moment cross our path and ask us: What are you going to do about me? When they ask it, they give us a moment of grace.

*Lewis B. Smedes,* A Pretty Good Person

The minister's morning toilet deserves consideration. I ask him to shave every day without exception, preferably early in the morning. I also ask him to dress carefully early in the morning. He should be carefully dressed always, unless he occasionally needs to don old clothes or overalls to do rough manual work. . . . Church members are not favorably impressed when they see their minister in all sorts of undress, wearing old slippers, lopping about collarless, even shirtless, hair unkempt. I knew a minister who answered his front door in his stocking feet.

*Walter E. Schuette,* The Minister's Personal Guide (1953)

Preacher, while you have no call to be a kill-joy when people are making merry at a happy wedding feast, neither have you the call to be the "life of the party."

. . . Your role at a wedding feast is not an easy one. Act it sympathetically, understandingly, and convincingly.

*Walter E. Schuette,* The Minister's Personal Guide (1953)

I affirm today that as far as the ministry is concerned, "I still hear trumpets in the morning."

*W. Frank Harrington*

Ministers become more and more preoccupied with trying to change society without changing the individual—whereas Jesus sought to change individuals, knowing that only through transformed and born-again people can society be changed.

*Agnes Sanford,* Sealed Orders

As a management consultant to churches, the most common problem I see among clergy is overwork or compulsive work.

*Speed B. Leas,* Time Management

The one piece of mail certain to go into my wastebasket is the letter addressed to the "busy pastor."

*Eugene H. Peterson,* The Contemplative Pastor

Teaching is, in my opinion, the most neglected dimension of the ministry today. Perhaps this neglect more than anything else accounts for the collective biblical and theological amnesia in the Church.

*James I. McCord*

Somehow, in most circles, no matter what the social standing of the deceased, no matter on which side of the railroad tracks death strikes, a minister is wanted at the funeral.

*Walter E. Schuette,* The Minister's Personal Guide (1953)

Taking souls from this world to heaven is God's main work, not ours. Our task is nurture not transportation. We are farmers not shippers.

*John K. Stoner,* Letters to American Christians

If there is one joke your pastor has heard before—and would be pleased to hear again—it is the joke about working only twenty minutes on Sunday morning.

*Robert G. Kemper,* What Every Church Member Should Know About Clergy

One of the afflictions of pastoral work has been to listen, with a straight face, to all the reasons people give for not going to church.

*Eugene H. Peterson,* A Long Obedience

# Quality of Character

Faith is the most important qualification of a leader.

*Arthur Merrihew Adams,* Effective Leadership

If asked to survey the church's leadership today, we would say, not that our clergy are not unfailingly polite, friendly, and cordial. They are cordial to a fault. The problem is, our clergy are not helping us get from one place to another. We are not sure that our clergy know where we are, much less where we ought to be, so how can they be expected to know what they should be doing?

*Stanley Hauerwas and William Willimon,* Resident Aliens

Courage, I have heard tell, is fear having said its prayers.

*Lewis B. Smedes,* A Pretty Good Person

Joy is not a requirement of Christian discipleship, it is a consequence.

*Eugene H. Peterson,* A Long Obedience

Joy, which was the small publicity of the pagan, is the gigantic secret of the Christian.

*G.K. Chesterton*

I have read that during the process of canonization the Catholic Church demands proof of joy in the candidate, and although I have not been able to track down chapter and verse I like the suggestion that dourness is not a sacred attribute.

*Phyllis McGinley,* Saint Watching

Leave sadness to those in the world. We who work for God should be light-hearted.

*Leonard of Port Maurice*

Christian leaders who like to think of themselves as so serious about justice, so concerned about the attainment of goodness, are often guilty of taking themselves too seriously, of ascribing too much good to their own efforts, their ideals, their righteous indignation.

*William Willimon,* The Laugh Shall Be First

Lord, shine in me and so be in me that all with whom I come in contact may know thy presence in my soul. Let them look up and see no longer me but only Jesus.

*John Henry Newman*

The humanity of ministers is often more difficult to perceive than that of lay people.

*Anonymous*

Growing in faith is not so much like going through stages as it is like exploring a new country. . . . There is always more to be seen and understood and taken in.

*Craig R. Dykstra*

I thank God for my handicaps, for through them I have found myself, my work, and my God.

*Helen Keller*

Waiting patiently in expectation is the foundation of the spiritual life.

*Simone Weil,* First and Last Notebooks

You cannot establish justice merely by condemning injustice. Neither can you create orthodoxy by condemning heresy. Righteousness and truth are the products of love rather than criticism.

*Thomas W. Gillespie*

Example is not the main thing in influencing others. It is the only thing.

*Albert Schweitzer*

Success is not measured by the heights one attains, but by the obstacles one overcomes in the attainment.

*Booker T. Washington*

Reputation is what people say about you.
Character is what God and your spouse know about you.

*Billy Sunday*

Character is what you have when you come to a new community.
Reputation is what you have when you go away.

*Anonymous*

# SUNDAY MORNING

# Proclaiming Good News

One might wonder how Jesus could ever use them [his disciples]. They were impulsive, temperamental, easily offended, and had all the prejudices of their environment. In short, these men selected by the Lord to be His assistants represented an average cross section of the lot of society in their day. Not the kind of group one would expect to win the world for Christ.

*Robert E. Coleman,* The Master Plan of Evangelism

This is our moment of history and our responsibility . . . to struggle for scriptural and practical means of what can be done in a fallen world to see people personally converted *and also* to see what our salt and light can bring forth in the personal life and the political and cultural life of this moment in history.

*Francis Schaeffer, in* Five Evangelical Leaders

How can we relate to people in a way that will change the world? Jesus did it in two ways: by his radical identification with men and women, and by his radical difference.

*Rebecca Manley Pippert,* Out of the Saltshaker and into the World

Somewhere, and I can't find where, I read about an Eskimo hunter who asked the local missionary priest, "If I did not know about God and sin, would I go to hell?" "No," said the priest, "not if you did not know." "Then why," asked the Eskimo earnestly, "did you tell me?"

*Annie Dillard*

One of Flip Wilson's unforgettable quips is this: "I'm a Jehovah's Bystander. They asked me to be a Witness, but I didn't want to get involved." Ultimately, as I see it, that is the fundamental issue. Do we want to get involved?

*Thomas W. Gillespie*

Laughter is a way of communicating joy, and joy is a net of love by which we can catch souls.

*Mother Teresa*

The churches that are growing today, as the churches of the Reformation, are clear as to the identity of the church and its minister. They did not and they do not confuse the church with a civic club, a social agency, or a political party; or the minister with a political operative, a therapist, or an executive.

*John H. Leith,* From Generation to Generation

Evangelism is not a labor reserved for clergy alone. In fact, the goal of church growth can almost be guaranteed if all members of congregations are united in the evangelism ministry.

*Clark Morphew*

We are better at talking about evangelism (in any style), than doing it.

*Thomas W. Gillespie*

To assure membership decline and loss of vitality:

- Don't post worship times on outdoor signs, so visitors have to work hard to find out when to come. Also, describe the church as a "family" church to discourage singles from worshiping.
- Never help newcomers lost in the order of worship. It's good for them to flounder.
- Make sure that only men serve as worship leaders so that women, young people, youth, and children feel left out.
- Sermons should: use words that people who didn't grow up in the church can't understand; use scholarly language that can't be understood by anyone except seminary graduates; use exclusive language, such as "mankind," so certain people feel left out.

- Welcome only people of your own race or those at or above your income level. This will keep your congregation "homogeneous." Be especially friendly to lawyers and doctors.
- Crowd into back pews so visitors have to be ushered up front and be stared at.
- Only official greeters should welcome visitors, because that's their job.
- Make building access difficult, to discourage the disabled from attending.
- Stare and glare to make newcomers feel uneasy and unwelcome.
- Never involve children and youth in worship or church life, as the church is only for adults.
- Members should gather in tight groups, and ignore visitors.

*Daniel W. Erlander,* Church of the Brethren Messenger

Behind all our thinking and planning, however, there must be a confidence that God is still at work in his world.

*David H.C. Read,* Go . . . and Make Disciples

Congregations will become healthier and more effective bearers of the divine presence when their sacramental life is renewed.

*Ben Campbell Johnson,* Rethinking Evangelism

Therefore go and make disciples of all nations, baptizing them in the name of the Father and of the Son and of the Holy Spirit, and teaching them to obey everything I have commanded you. And surely I am with you always, to the very end of the age.

*Matthew 28:19-20*

If Christians would really live according to the teachings of Christ, as found in the Bible, all of India would be Christian today.

*Mahatma Ghandi*

Contrary to our superficial thinking, there never was a distinction in His mind between home and foreign missions. To Jesus it was all world evangelism.

*Robert E. Coleman,* The Master Plan of Evangelism

It is a profound irony that the Son of God visited this planet and one of the chief complaints against him was that he was not religious enough.

*Rebecca Manley Pippert,* Out of the Saltshaker and into the World

The Spirit of Christ is the spirit of missions, and the nearer we get to Him the more intensely missionary we must become.

*Henry Martyn*

It is my conviction that rather than faith in a personal God being intellectually discredited, the reverse is the case. It is not that modern science has found Christian belief to be lacking an intellectual basis but, rather, when all the facts are considered together we begin to see atheism, unbelief, and materialism as the impostors they are.

*Archbishop George Carey,* Why I Believe in a Personal God

By love he may be caught but by thinking never.

*Unknown,* Cloud of Unknowing

It is actually all a supernatural performance and a supernatural process. All we are is witnesses to the saving grace and power of the Lord Jesus Christ. And I sincerely believe that any man preaching a simple gospel message in the power of the Spirit can expect results if he is speaking to unconverted people.

*Billy Graham, in* Five Evangelical Leaders

The reason some folks don't believe in missions is that the brand of religion they have isn't worth propogating.

*Anonymous*

The antihero for Christians is the American cowboy, out there dodging the arrows and bullets alone. Instead we are called to be a close family that welcomes the world into our midst. We invite people to come and share our love and our gifts. We are free to admit we have not arrived and are far from perfect. But because we believe Jesus is the living center of our group, we invite our non-Christian friends and acquaintances to hang around us and observe him.

*Rebecca Manley Pippert,* Out of the Saltshaker and into the World

# The Meaning of Ministry

The world is too bent for unshadowed joy. And yet, if we wait for every beggar to have his horse, we shall never be grateful for a ride. If we wait for every person to be fed, we shall never be grateful for our daily bread. If we wait for every person in the world to have a roof, we shall never be grateful for the roof that covers us as we sleep. If we wait till no one dies, we shall never feel grateful for life.

*Lewis B. Smedes,* A Pretty Good Person

It is high time the ideal of success should be replaced with the ideal of service.

*Albert Einstein*

Preachers may console themselves that no one is complaining. That's like the Commedia dell'Arte joke about the man who wanted to train his donkey to go without food. The donkey eventually died of starvation. "I have suffered a great loss," the man mourned. "Just when my donkey had learned the art of going without food, he died." Congregations, like the donkey, may not be complaining. That does not mean they are being trained to mediocrity. They may be just dying away.

*Michael Farrell*

Whatever you have received more than others—in health, in talents, in ability, in success, in a pleasant childhood, in harmonious conditions of home life—all this you must not take to yourself as a matter of course. In gratitude for your good fortune, you must render some sacrifice of your own life for another life.

*Albert Schweitzer*

With heavy theological luggage at the end of your arms, you will not be free to reach out to those who have none, or to assist those burdened by theirs, relieving them of guilty weight. And have you ever tried to hug someone with suitcases in your hands?

*Gail A. Ricciuti*

Nothing is more frustrating than to be afire with a cause and to discover that those around you do not share it. But to discover that others are constitutionally predisposed not to be set afire with any passion is enough to drive you up the wall. At no time do you so sense aloneness.

*Alfred Krass,* The Other Side

Unfortunately, the only language people really understand is their own language, and unless preachers are prepared to translate the ancient verities into it, they might as well save their breath.

*Frederick Buechner,* Whistling in the Dark

The test of a preacher is that his congregation goes away saying not, "What a lovely sermon" but, "I will do something!"

*St. Francis de Sales*

If you go against the grain of the universe, you get splinters.

*H.H. Farmer*

There is an emerging consensus that the most significant years of ministry for a pastor begin after the fourth to sixth year.

*John A. Esau,* Saying Good-bye

We think that we spend our lives serving others, but the Lord has a twofold plan. He wants us to learn how to serve others and become more like him. And then he turns around our serving and our situations to heal us, to care for us, and to grow us up, often through the very people we have helped!

*Jill Briscoe,* Renewal on the Run

There are many programs to prepare people for service in its different forms. But seldom do we look at these programs as a training toward a voluntary poverty. Instead we want to be better equipped and more skillful, we want to acquire the "tools of the trade." But real training for service asks for a hard and often painful process of self-emptying.

*Henri J.M. Nouwen,* Reaching Out

The first year they love you, the second year they hate you, the third year ministry begins.

*Anonymous*

Syrupy affection never yet led to spiritual integrity. And though it looks so like the charity which is greater than faith and hope that it is "admired of many," it is not admirable. It is sin. And it is blinding sin.

*Amy Carmichael,* Kohila

A ministry built on fear of the people can never be a healthy one.

*Stanley Hauerwas and William Willimon,* Resident Aliens

# The Sermon

Once congregations have heard good preaching of theological and biblical depth over a period of time, they find it difficult to accept poor preaching, or to be enticed by actors or entertainers or moral exhorters or therapists in the pulpit.

*John H. Leith*

On listening: at the University of Minnesota, hundreds of business and professional people were tested for their ability to grasp the content of short talks. The conclusion: Immediately after the average person has listened to someone, he remembers only about half of what was said, no matter how carefully he or she was listening. Within eight hours of hearing the short talk, only a quarter of what was said is remembered correctly.

*Unknown*

Unless the preacher has superb rhetorical skills, twenty minutes is about all that can be comfortably listened to.

*Homer K. Buerlein,* How to Preach More Powerful Sermons

Sermons and biscuits are improved by shortening.

*Anonymous*

A preacher who doesn't strike oil in 30 minutes should stop boring.

*Anonymous*

The most interesting point some preachers make is the stopping point.

*Anonymous*

Above all else, we must preach Christ . . . and not Christ in a vacuum . . . but rather a contemporary Christ who once lived and died, and now lives to meet human need in all its variety.

*John Stott*

The preacher who cannot broaden or deepen his sermons usually lengthens them.

*Anonymous*

A preacher should always stop preaching before the congregation stops listening.

*Anonymous*

43

Preaching is the most undemocratic of routines in a free society. Week in, week out, people come and listen for a half-hour at a time to someone like themselves. They do not interrupt; they do not walk out. They can't switch channels. Sometimes the speaker scolds them, and they sit still for it. They are not students in a university, intimidated by a professor's power over their marks and their futures; they are not employees dependent upon the speaker's power over their income. Many of them, in fact, are giving sacrificially to keep the speaker's family fed, clothed, housed, and educated. Those of us who have assumed such an undemocratic prerogative had better believe we are engaged in the ministry of the Word of God; otherwise there is no hope for us!

*Everett L. Wilson*

The minister who sets my teeth on edge is one who is trying a little too hard, has just a little too much heartiness coming from up front.

*Garrison Keillor*

My voice is really a half-octave too high for the ministry, though in praying aloud I have developed a way of murmuring to the lectern mike that answers to my amplified sense of the sililoquizing ego. My slight stammer keeps, they tell me, the pews from nodding.

*John Updike,* A Month of Sundays

Be careful not to preach more faith than you have.

*W. Frank Harrington*

Sermons are like women's skirts: they should be short enough to be interesting, but long enough to cover the subject.

*Anonymous (and should stay that way!)*

You know you're in trouble when the guest speaker begins with:
"A funny thing happened on the way to church this morning . . . "
"Unaccustomed as I am to public speaking . . . "
"Did you hear the one about the three ministers on an airplane . . . "
"Here are the notes for the sermon I was going to give, but I've decided not to give that message and simply say some things that need to be said . . . "
"As I was eating lunch with [insert big name] last week . . . "
"Webster defines [insert any word] as . . . "
"Yesterday's Cub's game has many parallels to this morning's text . . . "
"My wife doesn't like this sermon, but I decided to go ahead with it anyway . . . "
"This morning's message has eighteen points . . . "
"Last night I had a dream—of footprints in the sand . . . "
"Cereal boxes don't usually lead to sermon ideas, but this morning . . . "

"There are some topics that thirty minutes just can't do justice . . ."
"I was digging through some old seminary class notes this week . . ."
"At first glance, variants between the Septuagint and the Masoretic Text
    don't seem all that interesting, but . . ."
"Over the last few months, while struggling with my sexual identity . . ."
"I normally prepare my sermons in advance, but today . . ."

*Kevin Miller,* Leadership

To preach, to really preach, is to die naked a little each time and to know you
must do it again.

*Bruce Thielman*

I believe that abstractness in some ways is the greatest curse of all our
preaching; I speak as a great sinner in this respect.

*H.H. Farmer,* The Servant of the Word

Prophecy can explain only so much. Story telling is required for the rest.

*Garrison Keillor*

The pulpit is a terrible place to be if you have nothing to say.

*W. Frank Harrington*

A Scotch woman said to her minister, "I love to hear you preach. You get so many things out of your text that aren't really there."

*Watchman-Examiner*

I beg of you, study and pray for the power to break the umbilical cord between you and the word-by-word manuscript type of presentation.

*Homer K. Buerlein,* How to Preach More Powerful Sermons

Whoever first coined the phrase "an hour in the study for every minute in the pulpit" either never served a pastorate or, if he did, was surely admired by both of his members.

*Thomas G. Long,* The Senses of Preaching

Two views on what to preach away from one's own parish (take your pick):
    Never take new material on the road.
    Never ride an old horse out of town.

*Unknown*

Any fool can write learned jargon; the test is the vernacular.

*C.S. Lewis*

No sermon is ready for preaching, nor ready for writing out, until we can express its theme in a short, pregnant sentence as clear as crystal.

*H. Gerald Knoche*

Never use illustrations that swallow up sermons. Never use illustrations simply because they are so good they just have to be used. Never exegete illustrations. Avoid sentimental, "Reader's Digest" illustrations.

*John McClure,* Journal for Preachers

A true sermon is a tapestry drawn from tradition, memory, conversations long forgotten, candor, courtesy, pain and passion, fresh insight and fresh metaphor, but all united.

*Christine M. Smith,* Weaving the Sermon: Preaching in a Feminist Perspective

There once was an old man who had a particularly difficult time staying awake in church. In those days a warden walked the aisles with a long hickory rod, tapping anyone on the shoulder who went to sleep. One Sunday when the old man nodded off as usual during the sermon, the warden sternly tapped him on the shoulder with the rod. The old man kept on sleeping. The pastor frowned, and the warden tapped the man on the other shoulder with the rod. He still went on sleeping. The pastor shook his head and frowned again at the warden, and the warden took the long hickory rod and hit the man on the top of his head with it; whereupon the man fell out of the pew into the aisle, face down. He slowly opened one eye, squinted up at the warden, and said, "Hit me again. I can still hear him."

*Clyde E. Fant,* a sermon titled "On Getting the Last Laugh"

There's a big difference between having something to say and having to say something.

*Anonymous*

Never use a gallon of words to express a spoonful of thought.

*Anonymous*

In the Western world, the decline of preaching is a symptom of the decline of the church.

*John Stott*

Most people are bothered by those passages of Scripture they do not understand, but the passages that bother me are those I do understand.

*Mark Twain*

It is an awful responsibility to own a Bible.

*Anonymous*

It is no doubt a joy to the preacher to know that he is not only serving the same God as the saints of the past, but even using the time-honoured phrases which meant so much to them. But to his modern hearers (if they can be got within earshot!) he will only seem to be in love with the past. His words may have beauty and dignity, but it is the beauty and dignity of a past age; and his message often appears to be wholly irrelevant to the issues of today.

*J.B. Phillips,* Your God Is Too Small

The most privileged and moving experience a preacher can have is when, in the middle of a sermon, a strange hush descends upon the congregation. The sleepers have woken up, the coughers have stopped coughing, and the fidgeters are sitting still. No eyes or minds are wandering. Everybody is attending, though not to the preacher. For the preacher is forgotten, and the people are face to face with the living God, listening to his still, small voice.

*John Stott*

Sermons are like babies: easy to conceive, hard to deliver.

*Anonymous*

The best sermons I've heard, the ones that left me shaken afterward, always were based on simple story telling.

*Garrison Keillor*

# Money Matters

It is the things we cannot spare that make our offerings alive.

*Anonymous*

Money is a form of power. It is so intimately related to the possessor that one cannot consistently give money without giving self, nor can one give self without giving money.

*Anonymous*

Takers eat well; givers sleep well.

*Chi Chi Rodriguez, professional golfer*

Some people who give the Lord credit are reluctant to give him cash.

*Jack Herbert*

"Church administration" is simply a refined term for "raising money." It involves, of course, all sorts of activities—committee meetings, publicity, promotion, budget preparation, building supervision, public relations, etc., but it is all related to keeping your church solvent.

*Charles Merrill Smith,* How to Become a Bishop Without Being Religious

One reason we have so many pennies in the church collection plate is because we have no smaller coin.

*Anonymous*

Giving advice to the poor is about as near charity as some people ever get.

*Anonymous*

Mother: Quick, Henry, call the doctor. Johnny just swallowed a coin.
Father: I think we ought to send for the minister. He can get money out of anybody.

*Anonymous*

Money is an article which may be used as a universal passport to everywhere except heaven, and as a universal provider of everything except happiness.

*Anonymous*

You can't take your money to heaven, but you can send it on ahead.

*Anonymous*

No man is really consecrated until his money is dedicated.

*Roy L. Smith,* The Methodist Story

A painter in California was asked to contribute to a drive being conducted by his church. "I'm broke," he explained, "but I'll contribute a $300 picture."
When the drive was completed, the minister explained that it was still $100 short of the goal. "OK," said the artist. "I'll increase the price of my picture to $400."

*Anonymous*

Make all you can, save all you can, give all you can.

*John Wesley*

You haven't begun to give until you feel glad over it.

*Anonymous*

It's good to have money and the things that money can buy, but it's good, too, to check up once in a while and make sure that you haven't lost the things that money can't buy.

*George Horace Lorimer*

# Acts of Worship

The instinct to worship is hardly less strong than the instinct to eat.

*Dorothy Thompson*

It would look strange, indeed, were the minister to say, "Let us sing hymn number so-and-so," and then sit mute during the hymn singing. But I think it jars the average worshiper to have the minister sing lustily.

*Walter E. Schuette,* The Minister's Personal Guide (1953)

Bring an offering and come before him; worship the LORD in the splendor of his holiness.

*1 Chronicles 16:29*

The grace of worship is not that we are able to dance so well, but that God deigns to circle the floor with us in the first place.

*Thomas G. Long,* The Sense of Preaching

The test of a "successful" liturgy is not the feeling of euphoria and well-being that comes from a happy balance of readings well read, songs well sung, prayers well said, etc., but the pastoral and missionary activity of the community which follows from its worship.

*Anthony Boylan,* Symbolism and Liturgy

Obviously, unless the conception of God is something higher than a Magnification of our own Good Qualities, our service and worship will be no more and no less than the service and worship of ourselves. Such a god may be a prop to our self-esteem but is, naturally, incapable of assisting us to win a moral victory and will be found in time of serious need to fade disconcertingly away.

*J.B. Phillips,* Your God Is Too Small

I cannot fill the sanctuary with people, but I can fill the service with purpose. I cannot convince people they are sinners, but I can confess that I am a sinner. I cannot persuade the whole world, but I can proclaim the whole Word.

*Dick Rasanen*

Unless our feet are anchored in truth, it's very easy to go along with what is chic.

*Francis Schaeffer*

God's grace is greater than our gimmicks.

*David B. Watermulder*

Let the publicly praying minister bear in mind that God does not need a lot of detailed information; that at best it is difficult for worshipers to follow a spoken prayer and make it their own; and that, the longer he spins his prayers, the more certainly he destroys its benefit as far as his hearers, including God, are concerned.

*Walter E. Schuette,* The Minister's Personal Guide (1953)

The fewer the words the better the prayer.

*Martin Luther*

For where two or three come together in my name, there am I with them.

*Jesus Christ,* Matthew 18:20

The [person] who does not habitually worship is but a pair of spectacles behind which there is no eye.

*Thomas Carlyle*

Coming home from church one day, Emerson wrote, "The snow was real but the preacher spectral."

*Frederick Buechner,* Whistling in the Dark

Sunday rolls around with disturbing regularity.

*Fred R. Anderson*

CHURCH
LIFE

# That Mysterious Institution—The Church

The church is like Noah's ark: you couldn't stand the stink inside if you didn't know about the storm outside.

*Reinhold Niebuhr*

Many are in that uncertain state of health that makes them too frail to go to church on Sunday morning but just well enough to go for a joy ride Sunday afternoon.

*Anonymous*

Perhaps we forget, in a time of tame churches, toned down preachers, and accommodationist prophets, that there was a time when the church believed that though there was nothing in Jesus we needed to kill for, there was something here worth fighting for, dying for.

*Stanley Hauerwas and William Willimon,* Resident Aliens

The early Christians did not say to one another: Let us put up a building on the town square where we can hold services on Sunday morning at eleven o'clock and thereby get the spiritual dynamic to carry us through the week.

*Donald Macloed*

Mystery is a great embarrassment to the modern mind.

*Flannery O'Connor*

God help us, the one institution in the world most in danger of domesticating God and reducing him to a particular god of the in-group is the church . . . To think that God is our God is to violate everything the Bible affirms . . .

*Joseph A. Sanders,* God Has A Story Too

Too often we think of religion as a far off, mysteriously run bureaucracy to which we apply for assistance when we feel the need. We go to the branch office and direct the clerk (sometimes called a pastor) to fill out our order for God. Then we go home and wait for God to be delivered to us according to the specifications we have set down.

*Eugene H. Peterson,* A Long Obedience

Dearly beloved, let us open ourselves to this lesson. I feel you gathered beneath me, my docile suburban flock, sitting hushed in this sturdy edifice dedicated in the year 1883 and renovated under my canny predecessor in the year 1966. Strong its walls were built; with metal rods and extruded concrete were they reinforced. But let us pray together that its recollected and adamantine walls explode, releasing us to the soft desert air of this Sunday morning . . .

*John Updike,* A Month of Sundays

He who feeds his faith will starve his doubts to death.

*Vern McLellan*

When their religion becomes a succession of meetings and programs in which men and women address one another with pious phrases and solemn half-truths about God, when the basic convictions of the church are turned into slogans for stirring up bigger meetings with more eloquent addresses, Christian people begin to ask: "Is there nothing more to the Christian faith than this multiplicity of words?"

*Rachel Henderlite,* A Call to Faith

There is certainly nothing wrong with the church looking ahead, but it is terribly important that it should be done in connection with the look inside, into the church's own nature and mission, and a look behind at her own history. If the church does this, she is less likely to take her cues from the business community, the corporation, or the market place.

*Joseph Sittler*

There are thousands of local churches in the U.S., representing an enormous range of variation in doctrine and worship. Yet most define themselves as communities of personal support. . . . The salience of these needs for personal intimacy in American religious life suggests why the local church . . . is so fragile, requires so much energy to keep it going, and has so faint a hold on commitment when such needs are not met.

*Robert N. Bellah, et al,* Habits of the Heart

A high school stage play is more polished than this service we have been rehearsing since the year one. In two thousand years we have not worked out the kinks.

*Annie Dillard,* Pilgrim at Tinker Creek

The way of this world is to praise the dead saints and persecute the living ones.

*Anonymous*

For commonly, wheresoever God buildeth a church, the devil will build a chapel just by.

*Thomas Becon,* Catechism

This world is no friend to grace. A person who makes a commitment to Jesus Christ as Lord and Savior does not find a crowd immediately forming to applaud the decision nor old friends spontaneously gathering around to offer congratulations and counsel.

*Eugene H. Peterson,* A Long Obedience

The church must be a very strong and righteous thing, for it has survived every enemy it ever had.

*Eddie Cantor*

The chief trouble with the church is that you and I are in it.

*Charles H. Heimsath,* Sermons on the Inner Life

You and I are living in this evil hour in the history of the Christian church very largely because of what became of our grandfathers. They held onto their orthodoxy, but many of them had lost the life. The only way you can safeguard yourself from a dead orthodoxy is to put life even before orthodoxy. All appeals for unity in the New Testament are based on life.

*Martyn Lloyd-Jones*

One either confesses that God is the final authority or one confesses that Caesar is Lord.

*Francis Schaeffer*

Went to church today, and was not greatly depressed.

*Robert Louis Stevenson,* Journal

# Parish People

Now we ask you, brothers, to respect those who work hard among you, who are over you in the Lord and who admonish you. Hold them in the highest regard in love because of their work. Live in peace with each other.

*1 Thessalonians 5:12-13*

Some church members who say, "Our Father," on Sunday go around the rest of the week acting like orphans.

*Anonymous*

Church members who are pulling on the oars don't have time to rock the boat.

*Anonymous*

On complainers: Any jackass can kick down a barn that took ten good carpenters to build.

*A Texas rancher*

Nobody leaves the church. Let a guy have one chest pain, one twinge in the chest, and he goes flying back to the things he was taught in the third or fourth grade.

*Jimmy Breslin, syndicated newspaper columnist*

The person who is six days worldly and one day pious is, in fact, seven days worldly and not pious at all.

*Anonymous*

Most people who come to church want to know what you'll do for them, not what you'll ask them to do for others.

*Wallace E. Chappell, circuit rider*

It's not the difference between people that's the problem. It's the indifference.

*Anonymous*

We shall have to break our habit of having church in such a way that people are deceived into thinking that they can be Christians and remain strangers.

*Stanley Hauerwas and William Willimon,* Resident Aliens

Everyone says forgiveness is a lovely idea, until they have something to forgive.

*C.S. Lewis*

Always forgive your enemies—nothing annoys them so much.

*Oscar Wilde*

The trouble with some of us is that we have been inoculated with small doses of Christianity which keep us from catching the real thing.

*Anonymous*

Guess the weight of each member of the choir. This may be difficult since most choir robes look like Sears pup tents. Place bets and compare results with the person sitting next to you. Then, query each choir member after the service to determine who had the closest guess.

*Tim Sims and Dan Pegoda,* 101 Things To Do During A Dull Sermon

Religion in our time has been captured by the tourist mindset. Religion is understood as a visit to an attractive site to be made when we have the leisure. . . . We go to see a new personality, to hear a new truth, to get a new experience, and so, somehow, expand our otherwise humdrum lives. . . . We'll try anything—until something else comes along.

*Eugene H. Peterson,* A Long Obedience

We can't be blind to other people's faults; but we can be infinitely tender, comparing their worst with our worst and not their worst with our best.

*Anonymous*

Let us not give up meeting together, as some are in the habit of doing, but let us encourage one another—and all the more as you see the Day approaching.

*Hebrews 10:25*

The measure of a Christian is not in the height of his grasp but in the depth of his love.

*Clarence Jordan*

There is so much good in the worst of us, and so much bad in the best of us, that it hardly behooves any of us to talk about the rest of us.

*Anonymous*

A church membership does not make a Christian any more than owning a piano makes a musician.

*Douglas Meador,* These Times

In most congregations, and in nearly all small towns, the local grapevine is the most widely used channel of communication for disseminating reactions to the new minister.

*Lyle E. Schaller,* Getting Things Done

Judging from church attendance, heaven won't be packed with men.

*Anonymous*

[The pastor and pastor's spouse] are never viewed as being in the same category as "normal" people. Either people assume you are aloof or they themselves act aloof. Not only that, but people in a congregation . . . feel very intimidated and vulnerable when they see weaknesses in their "leaders" and those leaders' spouses. They are a little afraid to know what's really going on in our lives, especially if it's ugly, or it hurts. Somehow they think we should be "above" problems.

*Jill Briscoe,* Renewal on the Run

A Christian is the keyhole through which other folk see God.

*Robert E. Gibson*

# A Little Child Shall Lead Them

"Daddy, I want to ask you a question," said Jared after his first day in Sunday school.

"Yes, Son, what is it?"

"The teacher was reading the Bible to us—all about the children of Israel building the temple, the children of Israel crossing the Red Sea, the children of Israel making sacrifices. Didn't the grownups do anything?"

*Anonymous*

It is said that some Sunday-school children were once asked to write down their ideas as to what God was like. The answers, with few exceptions, began something like this: "God is a very old man living in Heaven . . ."! This is partly due to the fact that a child's superiors are always "old" to him and God must therefore be the "oldest" of all. . . . In addition to this his mind has quite probably been filled with stories of God's activities which happened "long ago." He is in consequence quite likely to feel, and even visualize, God as someone very old.

*J.B. Phillips,* Your God Is Too Small

## What Children Hear at Church

### *The Lord's Prayer:*
- How did you know my name? (or, Harold be thy name)
- Give us this day our jelly bread.
- Lead us not into Penn Station.
- Deliver us from people.

### *Hymn Titles and Lines from Hymns:*
- Gladly, the Cross-eyed Bear (Gladly, the Cross I Bear)
- Crazy, Crazy, All Ye Little Children, God Is Love . . . (Praise Him, Praise Him, All Ye Little Children, God Is Love)
- While Shepherds Washed Their Socks By Night (While Shepherds Watched Their Flocks By Night)
- Lead On, O Kinky Turtle (Lead On, O King Eternal)

The Sunday school teacher was describing how Lot's wife looked back and suddenly turned into a pillar of salt.

"My mother looked back once while she was driving," contributed little Heather, "and she turned into a telephone pole."

*Anonymous*

## Children On . . .

### *The Church Service*
- Mom, if you go to the circus, you'll never go to church again.
- I loved the music, but the commercial was too long.

### *Prayer*
- "Do you pray every night?" a little boy was asked. "No," he replied, "some nights I don't need anything."
- "I can't hear you," said a mother to her daughter who was praying. "I wasn't talking to you," came the reply.

### *Sunday School*
- "Dad, did you go to Sunday School?" asked the little boy.
  "Never missed a Sunday," was the answer.
  "Bet it won't do me any good either."
- My wife, who is a trial lawyer, opened her sixth-grade Sunday school class in prayer one morning with the words: "Your Honor, we give you thanks . . ." (It had been a long week in court.)

*Douglas J. Brouwer*

## More Children's Versions of the Lord's Prayer

- Our Father, Who are in heaven, hello! What be Thy name?
- Give us this day our daily breath.
- Our Father, Who are in heaven, Hollywood be Thy name.
- Lead us not into creation.
- Deliver us from eagles.
- "It's no use. Art doesn't listen to me," said a little girl who was praying for a bike. "Art who?" asked her mother. "Art in heaven," came the reply.

*Anonymous*

Sunday school teacher: What is prayer?
Student: That is a message sent to God at night and on Sundays when the rates are lower.

*Anonymous*

Sign on the door of a church nursery:
THEY SHALL NOT ALL SLEEP, BUT THEY SHALL ALL BE CHANGED!

The pastor was invited over for dinner and asked to lead in prayer before the meal. After the brief prayer, one of the children said: "You don't pray so long when you're hungry, do you?"

*Bob Phillips*

Dear God,
Are boys better than girls? I know you are one but try to be fair.
Sylvia

*Children's Letters to God*

A happy family is but an earlier heaven.

*Sir John Bowring*

On the way home from church a little boy asked his mother, "Is it true, Mommy, that we are made of dust?"
"Yes, darling."
"And do we go back to dust again when we die?"
"Yes, dear."
"Well, Mommy, when I said my prayers last night and looked under the bed, I found someone who is either coming or going."

*Unknown,* The World's Greatest Collection of Heavenly Humor

All preachers should steep themselves in good children's literature.

*Cornelius Plantinga, Jr.,* Reformed Journal

Dear God,
What is it like when you die? Nobody will tell me. I just want to know, I don't want to do it.
Your friend,
Mike

*Children's Letters to God*

# Denominational Differences

Christians may not always see eye-to-eye, but they can walk arm-in-arm.

*Anonymous*

During an inter-faith conference, someone shouted, "The building is on fire!"

Methodists gathered in a corner and prayed.

Baptists cried, "Where's the water?"

Quakers quietly praised God for the blessings fire brings.

Lutherans posted a notice on the door declaring, in no uncertain terms, that fire was evil.

Roman Catholics passed the offering plate to cover the damages.

Jews posted symbols on the doorposts hoping that the fire would pass over.

Congregationalists shouted, "Every man for himself!"

Fundamentalists proclaimed, "Fire is the vengeance of God!"

Christian Scientists agreed among themselves there was no fire.

Presbyterians appointed a chairperson who was to appoint a committee to look into the matter and make a written report to Session.

Episcopalians formed a procession and marched out.

*Unknown*

. . . if all the competing factions of Christendom were to give as much of themselves to the high calling and holy hope that unites them as they do now to the relative inconsequentialities that divide them, the Church would look more like the Kingdom of God for a change and less like an ungodly mess.

*Frederick Buechner,* Whistling in the Dark

Some people preserve their orthodoxy in vinegar.

*Anonymous*

What is the difference between a Presbyterian and a Mormon? A Presbyterian is one who knocks on your door and has nothing to say.

*Anonymous*

As long as Catholics marry Baptists, we'll have lots of Episcopalians.

*R. Roy Baines, Jr.*

How good and pleasant it is when brothers live together in unity!

*Psalm 133:1*

The thoughtful man outside the churches is not offended so much by the *differences* of denominations. To him . . . these are merely the normal psychological variations of human taste and temperament being expressed in the religious sphere. What he cannot stomach is the exclusive claim made by each to be the "right one." . . . If he were to observe the Church [making] the boldest and most exclusive claim . . . producing the finest Christian character, obviously wielding the highest Christian influence, and obviously most filled by the living Spirit of God—he could perhaps forgive the exclusive claim. *But he finds nothing of the kind.*

*J.B. Phillips,* Your God Is Too Small

Boy: "Dad, what is a backslider?"
Father: "A man who leaves our church and goes to another."
Boy: "And what is a man who leaves his church and joins ours?"
Father: "He's a *convert,* Son, a *convert.*"

*Anonymous*

Your own church steeple is not the only one that points to heaven.

*Anonymous*

Spero unitatem ecclesiarum (I hope for the unity of churches)
Spero pacen religionum (I hope for peace among religions)
Spero communitatem nationem (I hope for community among nations)
Where does the strength of my hope come from? For me personally, as for
millions of religious people around the world, the basis of my hope is that ut-
terly reasonable trust which is called faith.

*Hans Kung,* Reforming the Church Today

Religious differences are not nearly so disastrous as religious indifferences.

*Anonymous*

We are the precious chosen few:
Let all the rest be damned.
There's only room for one or two:
We can't have heaven crammed.

*Unknown*

People who fight fire with fire usually end up with ashes.

*Abigail Van Buren, advice columnist*

# Church Workers

Tact is the art of building a fire under people without making their blood boil.

*Anonymous*

The church has often been regarded as a haven for the emotionally disturbed. . . . Studies of the clergy are contradictory and emotionally charged. Overall, however, they suggest a high incidence of family problems and narcissistic disorders, and a host of other problems involving interpersonal relations and self-esteem . . .

*Thomas Maeder,* Atlantic Monthly

Team builders are the teabags of life. They are the people who perform when the water's hot.

*Roger Staubach, former professional football player*

The Peter Principle: In a hierarchy, every employee tends to rise to his level of incompetence (the cream rises until it sours).

*Peter and Hull,* The Peter Principle

The Peter Corollary: In time every post tends to be occupied by an employee who is incompetent to carry out its duties.

*Peter and Hull*, The Peter Principle

The person who writes the minutes controls the meeting.

*Anonymous*

A great deal can be done for the kingdom by "little servants" with "little skill" and "little training" if they have big hearts for God.

*Jill Briscoe*, Renewal on the Run

A committee is a group that keeps minutes and loses hours.

*Milton Berle*

After a lengthy meeting, one church's building committee set forth the following recommendations:
1. We will build a new church.
2. The new building is to be located on the site of the old one.
3. The material for the new building will come from the old one.
4. We will continue to use the old building until the new one is completed.

*Anonymous*

Everywhere I go it seems [church workers] are killing themselves with work, busyness, rushing, caring, and rescuing.

*Diane Fassel,* Working Ourselves to Death

There are many church officers who need to be fired—not out but up.

*Anonymous*

On meetings: Generally speaking, the fewer the better. Both as to the number of meetings and the number of participants.

*Robert Townsend,* Up the Organization

On supervising staff: It's easier to rein in a wild horse than it is to light a fire under a corpse.

*Fred R. Anderson*

A committee is a group of people who individually can do nothing, but who as a group can meet and decide that nothing can be done.

*Anonymous*

It's not whether you win or lose, but who gets the blame.

*Blaine Nye, former professional football player*

Tact is the ability to be brief, politely; to be aggressive, smilingly; to be emphatic, pleasantly; to be positive, diplomatically; to be right, graciously.
Tact is the art of making other people think they know more than you do.
Tact is the ability to stay in the middle without getting caught there.

*Franklin P. Jones*

We the unwilling
led by the unknowing
are doing the impossible
for the ungrateful.
We have done so much
for so long with so little,
we are now qualified
to do anything
with nothing!

*Unknown*

# On Seminary

For years my Bible class in Moorestown had prayed for seminaries, that they should teach the truth of the Gospels and send their young men forth to do the work that Jesus did. However, even to this day, I have seen very little answer to these prayers.

*Agnes Sanford,* Sealed Orders

On seminaries: . . . believing souls are trucked in like muddy, fragrant cabbages from the rural hinterland and in three years of fine distinctions and exegetical quibbling we have chopped them into cole slaw salable at any suburban supermarket. We take in saints and send out ministers, workers in the vineyard of inevitable anxiety and discontent.

*John Updike,* Roger's Version

Most of us enter a seminary with some very strong convictions which, in the course of a few years, get stretched, scrutinized, modified, or mangled, so that we are apt to emerge amazed at our own ignorance, and dripping with reservations about those things we most surely believed.

*David H.C. Read*

Preachers are the acid test of theology that would be Christian. Alas, too much theology today seems to have as its goal the convincing of preachers that they are too dumb to understand real theology.

*Stanley Hauerwas and William Willimon,* Resident Aliens

The popular preacher, Charles Spurgeon, was admonishing a class of divinity students on the importance of making the facial expressions harmonize with the speech in delivering sermons. "When you speak of heaven," he said, "let your face light up and be irradiated with a heavenly gleam. Let your eyes shine with reflected glory. And when you speak of hell . . . well, then your everyday face will do."

*Bob Phillips*

Student: Does a good beginning and a good ending make a good sermon?
Professor: If they're close enough together.

*Anonymous*

# From the Church Office

What to say if you're working in the church office and you answer the telephone (pick one):

He's not in yet.

I expect him any minute.

He just called to say he would be a few minutes late.

He was here, but he had to leave.

He went to lunch.

I expect him back from lunch any minute.

He's not back yet. May I take a message?

He's in the building, but not at his desk.

I'm not sure whether he'll be back or not.

Sorry, he's gone for the day.

*Anonymous*

# Some Words on Women

I do not believe that women have a right to be ministers. Neither do I believe that men have a right to be ministers. Ministry is not a matter of human rights but of divine decisions.

*Thomas W. Gillespie*

Christian ideology has contributed no little amount to the oppression of women.

*Simone deBeauvior,* Memoirs of a Dutiful Daughter

[Referring to seminary:] I have never been involved with an institution in which I was more aware of being female. . . . I think that I was supposed to get the message even before I got there.

*Susan C. Barrabee,* Education for Liberation

Clergywomen are less inclined [than men] to see themselves as authoritarian leaders set apart in status from lay people.

*Barbara J. MacHaffie,* Her Story

If the style of a woman's preaching was not to deliver (to proclaim) the Word but to place her ear close to the pulse of the people, then a new kind of Pentecost would be possible.

*Nelle Morton,* The Journey is Home

The major heresies of the church were, of course, launched by men.

*Ruth A. Tucker and Walter Liefeld,* Daughters of the Church

What about the one who buries someone else's talent? . . . Maybe we need to acknowledge the possibility that many of the people in our churches—the women—are not using their talents as they should, not necessarily because they don't want to but because they are not allowed to. If this is true, it is serious, especially for those who might be doing the burying.

*Stuart Briscoe*

Neither reason nor Christianity invites women to the professor's chair, nor conducts her to the bar, nor makes her welcome to the pulpit, nor admits her to the place of ordinary magistracy.

*John Angell James,* Female Piety (1858)

Sin began with a woman,
And because of her we all die.
Do not give water an outlet
Nor a wicked woman freedom to speak.
If she does not act as you would have her,
Cut her off from your person.

*The Wisdom of Sirach (the Apocrypha)*

Theologians of the early church had no difficulty imagining a heaven inhabited solely by males [because] when we got there we [women] were changed into men.

*Mary Pellauer*

The time has come to declare that since the public activity of a woman is no longer considered a breach of the marriage vow and since the law of the land no longer denies to women the right to act independently in promiscuous gatherings, women are eligible candidates for any office in the Church of Christ if, of course, they have qualifications equal to male candidates for the office.

*Russell C. Prohl,* Women in the Church (1957)

## From the Parsonage

How many reproductions of Albrecht Durer's "The Praying Hands" can be displayed in one home? Since my husband's ordination, some of our friends have felt the necessity for giving us "religious art." Although we deeply appreciate their thoughtfulness and generosity, no black velvet paintings of "The Last Supper" will ever hang on the wall behind our sofa.

*Judith J. Koch,* Lutheran Partners

The doctor or dentist or lawyer or accountant or mechanic goes home from patients, clients, or customers. The pastor goes home from brothers and sisters in Christ. They are intense competition for sons and daughters and spouse. There is only one way to keep the church family from winning. It is to cut one's own family into one's schedule with a blowtorch.

*Robert Hudnut,* This People, This Parish

If you work with youth they *will* need to be in your home. This doesn't mean you shouldn't attempt to corral them. I remember putting a big sign on the bottom of the stairs that said, "Where do you think you're going?" It didn't

stop them from spreading all over the house, but at least it was an attempt—
it made *me* feel better. This is part of what it means to love strangers.

*Jill Briscoe,* Renewal on the Run

A minister habitually told his congregation that if they needed a pastoral visit
to drop a note in the offering plate. One evening after services he discovered
a note that said: "I am one of your loneliest members and heaviest contribu-
tors. May I have a visit tomorrow evening?" It was signed by his wife.

*Anonymous*

More perfect to me than the praise, "You entertain beautifully!" is the whis-
per of the young girl who had just come to know Christ, "Thank you for having me. God is here in this home."

*Karen Burton Mains*

Living the way we assume other people think we should live can be exhaust-
ing.

*Ruth Senter*

# Memorable Church Signs

For God so loved the world that He didn't send a committee.

*(Benton, Wisconsin)*

The competition is terrible, but we're still open for business.

*(Evergreen Park, Illinois)*

Last chance to pray before entering the tollway.

*(Dallas, Texas)*

Had a tough week? We're open Sundays.

*(Wheaton, Illinois)*

If you have troubles, come in and tell us about them.
If you have none, come in and tell us how you do it.

*(Denver, Colorado)*

Heaven knows when you were here last.

*(Baton Rouge, Louisiana)*

Come in and pray today. Beat the Christmas rush.

*(Los Angeles, California)*

Keep off the grass. This means thou.

*(Des Moines, Iowa)*

All new sermons! No re-runs!

*(Shrevesport, Louisiana)*

Come early . . . if you want a back seat.

*(Hopewell, New Jersey)*

The Lord loveth a cheerful giver; He accepteth from a grouch.

*(Kansas City, Missouri)*

Come in and let us prepare you for your finals.

*(Ann Arbor, Michigan)*

Start living to beat hell.

*(Wilkes Barre, Pennsylvania)*

Come in and have your faith lifted.

*(Unknown)*

Do come in—Trespassers will be forgiven.

*(Bronx, New York)*